D0717350

Some things are
sometimes yellow...

Some things are
usually yellow...

Some things are
almost always yellow...

What yellows do you see?

DK

A DORLING KINDERSLEY BOOK

First published in Great Britain by Dorling Kindersley Limited
Copyright © 1993 Dorling Kindersley Limited
Colour reproduction by Colourscan, Singapore
Printed in Singapore by Tien Wah Press Ltd

Yellow

DORLING KINDERSLEY

LONDON • NEW YORK • STUTTGART

banana

chick

daffodil

sweetcorn

bath duck

sponge

lemon

sailing
boat

sunflower

cheese

pepper

mittens

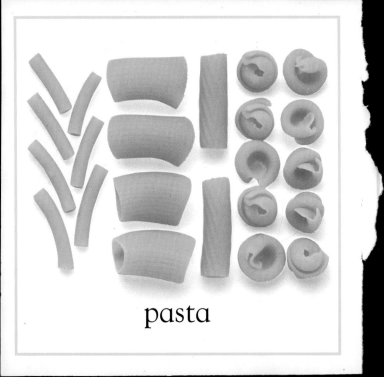

pasta

grapefruit

canary

ribbon